SARCASTIC

Daily Meditations

- Precisely what is **Untrue** -

365 Days A Year

By "Clay F"

www.sarcasticbigbook.com

INSTAGRAM: @sarcastic.aa.book

JANUARY 1ST

This year, make sure it's your words, and not your actions, that speak for you

JANUARY 2ND

God probably saved you from the throes of addiction so you could lie on the couch all day and gaze at your cellphone

JANUARY 3RD

*Do not thank anyone for
the countless things that
will go right today*

JANUARY 4TH

If there's one thing this world needs today, more than ever, it's another person telling everyone else what they need to do

JANUARY 5TH

There are really no words for how good it feels to receive unsolicited advice

JANUARY 6TH

Everything has to go exactly as you plan it today, or there's probably no God

JANUARY 7TH

Today, see that your significant other watches the shows you feel like watching. Your wants and needs are more important

JANUARY 8TH

No one wants to hear that they are trying their best, and that they are doing a great job

JANUARY 9TH

Don't say "I Love You" again to someone if you've already said it at some point

JANUARY 10TH

Mentally clock out when you get home from work and finally with your family. They certainly haven't done anything that would warrant having you at your best

JANUARY 11TH

Throughout this day, remind yourself that your experience is just always much more important than anyone else's

JANUARY 12TH

Only be nice to people if you're in a good mood. That makes sense and seems fair

JANUARY 13TH

It is rational to talk shit about the person you've chosen to be with

JANUARY 14TH

When someone enjoys something that you don't like, say insulting things about it

JANUARY 15TH

Never say hi to cashiers. They're not real human beings. Just place your order

JANUARY 16TH

Today, set the bar low for yourself and wave the flag of mediocrity

JANUARY 17TH

Since it feels so good to be micromanaged, do it to others as often as possible. It puts people at ease and brings out their best

JANUARY 18TH

Fixate on tomorrow, because tomorrow has been promised

JANUARY 19TH

Beat yourself up about the things you did wrong yesterday. It makes a big difference

JANUARY 20TH

*What matters the most
is how spiritual you
sound to other people*

JANUARY 21ST

Thought for today: "This year has barely begun and already things have turned to complete shit. Since my perspective has nothing to do with it, I should probably just give up"

JANUARY 22ND

*People feel closer to you
when you yell*

JANUARY 23RD

*Nothing on this planet got done
correctly before you were born*

JANUARY 24TH

Your opinion is usually crucial

JANUARY 25TH

Your life was probably saved so you could spend about four hours a day masturbating to hardcore pornography

JANUARY 26TH

It's probably God's will that you bond with others over negativity

JANUARY 27TH

*If you owe someone an apology,
don't be in any kind of hurry.
Just get around to it someday*

JANUARY 28TH

Take yourself extremely seriously today. It feels good, and other people love it

JANUARY 29TH

Being irresponsible does not cause anxiety

JANUARY 30TH

The more you think about yourself, the happier you'll be

JANUARY 31ST

Always remember that the people around you are basically fucked without your two cents

FEBRUARY 1ST

True freedom comes from avoiding responsibility

FEBRUARY 2ND

Today, fixate on all that could go wrong. There's so much!

FEBRUARY 3RD

You're not doing the right thing because you don't know what the right thing is! It's not like you know exactly what the right thing is and you just don't wanna do it or anything

FEBRUARY 4TH

*People emotionally embrace
those who are never wrong
about anything*

FEBRUARY 5TH

Just can't stress enough how important it is to be right about everything. *People love it so much*

FEBRUARY 6TH

No one could ever possibly underscore enough how fucking important it is to be right all the time

FEBRUARY 7TH

*A constant, relentless,
seemingly endless analyzation
of one's defects brings both
peace and answers*

FEBRUARY 8TH

*Concentrate on planning what
you are going to say while
other people are talking*

FEBRUARY 9TH

*You were probably saved from
the throes of addiction so you
could start debates that leave
everyone feeling distant and sad*

FEBRUARY 10TH

*Only pick up trash if
someone's looking*

FEBRUARY 11TH

You were probably given another shot at life so you could bitch and complain all day

FEBRUARY 12TH

Everyone is thinking about you right now

FEBRUARY 13TH

Today's goal: concentrate on being understood

FEBRUARY 14TH

Rules totally matter and everything, but if you don't want them to apply to you, that's fine. Fuck it

FEBRUARY 15TH

Life isn't hard enough all on its own already. See if you can make the lives of others even more challenging

FEBRUARY 16TH

If you just think really, really hard, your behavior will change

FEBRUARY 17TH

You were probably saved
from the throes of addiction
so you could be #1 at every
single thing you touch

FEBRUARY 18TH

Speak about everything with authority, whether you know what you're talking about or not

FEBRUARY 19TH

Maybe God reached into the pit of hell, lifted you up and out, and placed you on your high horse

FEBRUARY 20TH

Today, kids desperately need more big shots to look up to

FEBRUARY 21ST

Today, do whatever you can to try and make other people feel that you're just a little bit better than them

FEBRUARY 22ND

The world owes us something

FEBRUARY 23RD

As long as the pillows on your couch have things about love and laughter written all over them, it's totally okay that you act like a piece of shit

FEBRUARY 24TH

You're the only one who understands exactly how today is supposed to unfold

FEBRUARY 25TH

You're smarter than anyone else, and no one can tell when you're being manipulative

FEBRUARY 26TH

Being a control freak just means that you like everything to go smoothly for you, and for everyone around you. There's nothing more to it

FEBRUARY 27TH

Your intentions are everything. What you actually do is just whatever

FEBRUARY 28TH

You're done. There's really nothing more you could be doing to try to grow today

MARCH 1ST

*You can't do things
that are difficult*

MARCH 2ND

Something being hard to do
is a good reason to not do it

MARCH 3RD

You were probably saved from crippling addiction so you could have a so-so life

MARCH 4TH

Things in and of themselves are special. It has nothing to do with the meaning we assign

MARCH 5TH

The stars are so high up there. Today, aim for, like, the top of a medium-sized tree

MARCH 6TH

Once you've been clean and sober for a few weeks, you're ready to start dating

MARCH 7TH

Don't waste any of your time celebrating people who are still alive

MARCH 8TH

Spend as much time as you can hanging out with people who drag you down. We're all promised long lives and this kind of crap can be sorted out later

MARCH 9TH

*God's plan was probably to a)
save your life, b) put you on a
beautiful, positive course, and
then c), just let it all crumble
apart in slow motion*

MARCH 10TH

As long as you spend some time each week sitting in a yoga pose, how you interact in your personal relationships will never matter much

MARCH 11TH

*No one else's time should
be viewed as precious*

MARCH 12TH

You'd be so much happier if people would do things your way. Because happiness is a byproduct of having things go your way

MARCH 13TH

Find someone willing to help you, summon up the courage to ask them for help, and then reject their suggestions

MARCH 14TH

Feelings are always brilliant;
never question them at all

MARCH 15TH

You were probably given a second chance at life so that you could act like a revolting predator

MARCH 16TH

Do a really *half-assed job today!*

MARCH 17TH

What you say to a person's face is what matters. What you say behind their back doesn't matter at all, and it says nothing about you

MARCH 18TH

Gossiping about other people is about you trying to be helpful, and has nothing to do with your own insecurities

MARCH 19TH

Do a ho-hum job at work today and then complain about what they pay you

MARCH 20TH

What the people who really love you care the most about is the kind of car you drive

MARCH 21ST

*Everyone benefits from you
talking more than them*

MARCH 22ND

Only text someone if you need something from them. It's completely understandable that you're too busy to say hi or something

MARCH 23RD

Since you have never made any mistakes, you are in a position to judge other people

MARCH 24TH

*The meaning of life probably
has something to do with
an ongoing withholding
of love from others*

MARCH 25TH

You have to be perfect today. Perfectionism usually comes off as very healthy, and the people around you absolutely love it

MARCH 26TH

Give God advice

MARCH 27TH

Too much has probably been made of the value of friendliness and manners

MARCH 28TH

If someone is not doing it the way you believe it should be done, it just means that life is unfair

MARCH 29TH

If someone else is talking, and you personally don't give a shit about what they're saying, make that obvious through your body language

MARCH 30TH

Lie about who you are to the people you date

MARCH 31ST

Actually, lie about who you are to everyone, as long as it helps you get what you want from them

APRIL 1ST

A common thing you'll hear at funerals is, "I always loved that my parent was a workaholic"

APRIL 2ND

*Be true to yourself unless
it bothers other people*

APRIL 3RD

*The internal conversations
you have with yourself
only vaguely contribute to
the shaping of your life*

APRIL 4TH

*Pick someone to be with,
complain about them, and
then give them your worst*

APRIL 5TH

You can't try harder

APRIL 6TH

Children love being in the company of bitter adults

APRIL 7TH

Self-righteousness attracts all the right people

APRIL 8TH

If someone treats you poorly today, you should treat other people poorly

APRIL 9TH

You deserve to be treated
better *than other people.*
Don't forget that

APRIL 10TH

It should be up to you when and if people forgive you for the stuff you've done that has hurt them

APRIL 11TH

As long as you say the right things, do whatever you want

APRIL 12TH

*What you do does not impact
a whole bunch of people*

APRIL 13TH

You were likely saved from the throes of addiction so you could regularly deceive other people regarding your motives

APRIL 14TH

*Now that you're sober,
don't go above and beyond.
In fact, try to put off the
same kind of energy that
probably slowly kills plants*

APRIL 15TH

Cynicism never has anything to do with being hurt in the past. A cynical person is just way smarter than you, and they've seen more

APRIL 16TH

When you talk shit about people behind their backs, everyone trusts you more

APRIL 17TH

If you are in any way helpful to someone, never let them hear the end of it

APRIL 18TH

If you talk more than everyone else, it just means that you have more important things to say than everyone else

APRIL 19TH

Don't thank people too often, if at all, because you're entitled to the kindness around you

APRIL 20TH

Your conscience is dumb

APRIL 21ST

*It's not selfish to be nicer
to people you'd
consider fucking*

APRIL 22ND

You are responsible for the choices that other people make

APRIL 23RD

If you are a bully, it only means that you know more, and that you are stronger

APRIL 24TH

Your loved ones probably planned that intervention so that you could be enabled by insurance companies, make fun of 12-Step programs, and have sex with strangers

APRIL 25TH

When you're bored, it has nothing to do with the fact that you're only thinking about you

APRIL 26TH

Do not honor others by beginning conversations with a hello of any kind. Just get right into what you need from them

APRIL 27TH

Once a certain amount of time goes by, you're really done growing spiritually

APRIL 28TH

Your very life was probably saved so you could sleep with people you don't really care about

APRIL 29TH

*It's valuable to talk down
to yourself about stuff*

APRIL 30TH

When you beat yourself up, it really helps the people around you

MAY 1ST

If someone else is celebrating something, find a way to make it about you

MAY 2ND

Come out on top somehow in every conversation you have. People will like you more

MAY 3RD

*No one sees through you
to your real motives*

MAY 4TH

*How you handle things when
they don't go your way says
very little about you*

MAY 5TH

Where there is darkness, try to bring even more darkness

MAY 6TH

*Where there is truth,
bring error*

MAY 7TH

*Where there is harmony,
bring confusion*

MAY 8TH

Where there is misunderstanding, try and bring even more of that

MAY 9TH

Just for today - try staying in your own head, so you can accidentally contribute to the discord that surrounds you, all day long

MAY 10TH

Since you yourself have never fucked up, if someone else makes a mistake, make them feel like shit about it

MAY 11TH

Don't accept genuine apologies unless they are precisely the kind that you yourself give

MAY 12TH

Greet fear with fear

MAY 13TH

Your life was probably saved so that you could be really hard on other people

MAY 14TH

*There are unselfish reasons
to withhold empathy*

MAY 15TH

Compassion has a ceiling

MAY 16TH

There are already too many people in the world trying to be a little bit nicer today

MAY 17TH

It is wise to dwell on your past achievements

MAY 18TH

True happiness is a byproduct of watching tv

MAY 19TH

*Concentrate on what other
people need to change*

MAY 20TH

The less synced up your inner dialogue is with what you actually say, the more you'll like yourself

MAY 21ST

We deserve grace

MAY 22ND

Wait until everyone else is being good to you before you start being good to anyone else

MAY 23RD

Levity has no spiritual value

MAY 24TH

Children are usually born depressed - and then adults cheer them up, and they just become happier and happier and happier

MAY 25TH

If "Higher Power" means a power that is higher than you, there's just no way one could exist

MAY 26TH

*When your thoughts
are judgemental, you're
just more free*

MAY 27TH

People who always need to know what's going on with everyone else are usually very comfortable with themselves

MAY 28TH

Take relationship advice from people in unhappy relationships

MAY 29TH

It's unhealthy to laugh at yourself. Tighten up

MAY 30TH

*Insult things that hold
meaning to your loved ones*

MAY 31ST

Remember that love is a noun

JUNE 1ST

You were probably yanked from the alcoholic pit of despair so that you could bring a shitty attitude into some workplace today

JUNE 2ND

If you can't think of things for which to be grateful, it just means that there aren't any

JUNE 3RD

When you repeatedly tell yourself that you're incapable of getting out of self, it springs you into growth

JUNE 4TH

When you concentrate on outward appearances you reach people's hearts

JUNE 5TH

Make sure that your body is ripped; it doesn't matter whether or not your soul is flabby and gross

JUNE 6TH

Your problems are the
most important problems
to other people

JUNE 7TH

*Live today as if you were going
to be around for about
a hundred years*

JUNE 8TH

If you think something nice about somebody, just keep it to yourself

JUNE 9TH

*If you want your soul to soar,
seek out people who like to brag*

JUNE 10TH

Who you choose to hang out with doesn't say anything important about you

JUNE 11TH

Do not honor yourself if a toxic person takes issue with it

JUNE 12TH

Every challenge you will ever face is only there to keep you down

JUNE 13TH

How you deal with stuff is irrelevant because, eventually, everything will just start going your way permanently

JUNE 14TH

Focus on maintaining an environment where people are afraid to be themselves around you

JUNE 15TH

Your children only pay attention to your words

JUNE 16TH

It takes a lot of effort to take someone for granted

JUNE 17TH

People are way too distracted by what you're saying to notice what you're doing

JUNE 18TH

*Don't worry about trying
to do anything differently
today. You just can't*

JUNE 19TH

People who act like they are superior to others have hardly any insecurities

JUNE 20TH

*It is freeing to the human spirit
to bond with others over all
that is wrong with this world*

JUNE 21ST

Anger is a primary emotion, and has nothing to do with being hurt or afraid

JUNE 22ND

Don't make deliberate attempts to celebrate the partner you have chosen

JUNE 23RD

Whenever you know anything about the topic being discussed, chime in and tell all, a hundred percent of the time, no matter what

JUNE 24TH

*Communicate less and less
with the people who have a
healthy influence on you*

JUNE 25TH

You were likely saved from the throes of addiction so you could cram your opinion down the throats of others

JUNE 26TH

Where there is hope, try to bring a little despair

JUNE 27TH

Know that no one else has any pain that would be helpful for them to talk about

JUNE 28TH

It's loving to trick people

JUNE 29TH

Don't ever consider the kind of day someone else is having. It should never even be on your radar. Just go up to them and unload about whatever may be pissing you off

JUNE 30TH

It's probably God's will to bash things that are loved by your spouse

JULY 1ST

*Everyone in your life will
100% be there tomorrow*

JULY 2ND

Be critical of free help

JULY 3RD

*Never thank anyone for jobs
that are normally thankless*

JULY 4TH

The true purpose of an intimate relationship probably has something to do with feeding your ego

JULY 5TH

Thought for the day: Sure, children are the future. But fuck stopping at lemonade stands

JULY 6TH

Your life was probably saved so you could remain in relationships based on fear

JULY 7TH

Whether or not other people
change is up to you

JULY 8TH

God probably gave you brains so that you could rely on the opinions of manipulative people

JULY 9TH

Honor a person who is talking by making it clear that you're listening to them, unless there's something more interesting to look at on your phone

JULY 10TH

Let unhappy people guide you through life and you will end up happy

JULY 11TH

Treat the people you care about the most the worst

JULY 12TH

What you eat is more important to your soul than what you watch

JULY 13TH

No child in your life needs to see a healthy adult relationship modelled

JULY 14TH

No one is going through more than you are

JULY 15TH

In life, be like a golden retriever - if someone feeds you, give them affection and wag your tail. If someone robs your house, give them affection and wag your tail

JULY 16TH

Maybe your life was saved so you could become freaking amazing at blowing enormous vape clouds

JULY 17TH

Another common thing you hear at funerals: "My fondest memory was the size of the house"

JULY 18TH

Chances are good that most of the things you're worrying about right now will be just as relevant this time next month

JULY 19TH

*Other people will be responsible
for how you behave today*

JULY 20TH

You are definitely the person who should decide what is appropriate for everyone else

JULY 21ST

It would take too long to text "I love you" to someone randomly today, so don't do it

JULY 22ND

It feels good when someone only contacts you when they need something

JULY 23RD

*If you have a bad moment,
make sure it destroys an
hour. Or a whole day*

JULY 24TH

If your first thought is, "I don't want to", then you should never volunteer to help anyone

JULY 25TH

*Be critical of people who
are being vulnerable*

JULY 26TH

Make it your job to always correct the people around you. They will feel safer to be themselves

JULY 27TH

If someone else is trying to do something that you've never done, make sure that you're opinionated about it

JULY 28TH

The world will be going in the wrong direction until there are more successful businesses

JULY 29TH

You are incapable of being a big influence

JULY 30TH

No one around you would feel any happier if you tried to be more loving today

JULY 31ST

Once you're not a little kid anymore, your heart doesn't need anyone to be more gentle

AUGUST 1ST

*The things that are just
handed to us will
always mean the most*

AUGUST 2ND

Honor people, not principles

AUGUST 3RD

God's voice is probably manic

AUGUST 4TH

Look in the mirror, and say this to yourself: "You're the best judge of what someone else needs to do"

AUGUST 5TH

Pray.
But as soon as you open
your eyes, play God

AUGUST 6TH

*Real strength means being
afraid to ask for help*

AUGUST 7TH

There's nothing selfish about giving someone the silent treatment

AUGUST 8TH

Admitting when you're wrong creates a distance between you and God

AUGUST 9TH

Deep inside, you don't know the difference between right and wrong

AUGUST 10TH

Brutal honesty rarely hurts people, so it's rarely unloving

AUGUST 11TH

You're the only person who thinks they're smarter than other people

AUGUST 12TH

We feel so much closer to people who are never wrong

AUGUST 13TH

You'll get another chance at living this day

AUGUST 14TH

If you're afraid to do something it simply means that you shouldn't do it

AUGUST 15TH

You'll reach great heights by trying really hard up until you hit a roadblock of some kind

AUGUST 16TH

Make your mantra "I understand everything"

AUGUST 17TH

Anxiety will help prevent most uncomfortable things from happening to you

AUGUST 18TH

Discourage people who are making progress if they're not making it as fast as you think they should

AUGUST 19TH

Only a small portion of what you do impacts others

AUGUST 20TH

The slower you are to forgive, the better

AUGUST 21ST

If you fear spontaneity, it only means that you are very organized and orderly, and that you like to plan things

AUGUST 22ND

If the entire world were watching you on television, most would totally understand why you complain

AUGUST 23RD

If someone brings up something with which you are familiar, just unload everything you know about it on them right away before they can even get a word in edgewise

AUGUST 24TH

*Concentrate primarily
on the love you receive
and you'll be happier*

AUGUST 25TH

"Because other people are doing it" is an excellent reason to do something

AUGUST 26TH

You're probably useful to your Higher Power when you're thinking about how much you've been screwed over by life

AUGUST 27TH

People hear it often enough that they are appreciated

AUGUST 28TH

*Focus on asking yourself
the questions that can
never really be answered,
and are also irrelevant*

AUGUST 29TH

It takes thirty seconds to write a love note to your spouse, and that's thirty seconds you don't have

AUGUST 30TH

There's just no way you're capable of loving people any better than you already are

AUGUST 31ST

*Your life was probably saved
so you could do the same
shit over and over again and
pretend that you're confused*

SEPTEMBER 1ST

What you get from others today should determine how good your day is

SEPTEMBER 2ND

Once you're in a committed relationship, the real spiritual work for you is pretty much over

SEPTEMBER 3RD

*If you want to grow quickly,
judge yourself harshly*

SEPTEMBER 4TH

You were probably saved from the throes of addiction so you could pound energy drinks and exchange DNA with people you won't know this time next year

SEPTEMBER 5TH

People only deserve your best at the beginning of the relationship

SEPTEMBER 6TH

If there's something you're hiding from people you pretend to be close to, don't examine that

SEPTEMBER 7TH

Selfishness is rarely covert

SEPTEMBER 8TH

Due to the mere fact that you were born, you just deserve a bunch of stuff

SEPTEMBER 9TH

*When you start a sentence
with, " What you need
to do is…" , it makes the
person you're talking to
more open-minded*

SEPTEMBER 10TH

When you are uncomfortable because someone else is not doing what you think they should be doing, it is usually just an indication that you are being truly loving

SEPTEMBER 11TH

If your real objective is to be helpful to a person, speak with aggression and judgement

SEPTEMBER 12TH

The world needs more people to come off as self-righteous

SEPTEMBER 13TH

If it's just based on how we drive, people are getting nicer and nicer

SEPTEMBER 14TH

If you're clean and sober now, and there are people who still don't trust you, they are way off

SEPTEMBER 15TH

No one else has ever had the kind of fears that you have

SEPTEMBER 16TH

Everybody knows what
they're doing except for you

SEPTEMBER 17TH

If you really want anything to change, don't allow yourself to be challenged by people you trust

SEPTEMBER 18TH

Never think about whether you're being a good or bad influence on people. It doesn't matter

SEPTEMBER 19TH

*Trying to become more patient
is a waste of your energy*

SEPTEMBER 20TH

Whenever you disagree with something, it's important that you express it

SEPTEMBER 21ST

The purpose of life is probably that we encounter some trouble and then just be sort of stuck there

SEPTEMBER 22ND

Everyone else is just about to start doing things your way

SEPTEMBER 23RD

You're the only person on this planet thinking about themselves right now

SEPTEMBER 24TH

If you have some unresolved stuff going on, becoming more uptight about it usually does the trick

SEPTEMBER 25TH

You should only be nice to people when you feel good

SEPTEMBER 26TH

It's hard to look for things that are wrong.
It's way easier to look for things that are right

SEPTEMBER 27TH

Assume that your experience in any given moment is the exact same as everyone else's

SEPTEMBER 28TH

The opinions of complete strangers online should be the most valuable to you

SEPTEMBER 29TH

The people that you know are more intelligent than your conscience

SEPTEMBER 30TH

When you tell people what to believe, it empowers them

OCTOBER 1ST

You can remain in relationships that are terrible for your soul, as long as you regularly attend pilates classes

OCTOBER 2ND

Now that you're finally sober you can let everyone else know what the hell they're doing wrong

OCTOBER 3RD

People just love you more when you try to prove that you're capable of solving absolutely everything on your own

OCTOBER 4TH

You're the only person in your life who feels under-appreciated

OCTOBER 5TH

The strongest people on the planet are the ones who never cry

OCTOBER 6TH

If you only try to control people and situations and information covertly, from behind the scenes, then you're not manipulative

OCTOBER 7TH

You are too unintelligent to know when you're just making up an excuse for something

OCTOBER 8TH

*The wisest souls talk
over children*

OCTOBER 9TH

Help only when it's convenient for you

OCTOBER 10TH

How you drive says nothing about your awareness of the experience of others

OCTOBER 11TH

Today, just phone it in.
No one will notice

OCTOBER 12TH

It takes two seconds to tell someone that you care about them, so rarely bother with this

OCTOBER 13TH

There will be time later on

OCTOBER 14TH

During tragedies, people are usually put in touch with the most irrelevant things about life

OCTOBER 15TH

When you close your heart off to "protect" yourself, you only block the bad things

OCTOBER 16TH

Fear teaches beautiful things

OCTOBER 17TH

Cynicism has nothing to do with the health of one's own motives

OCTOBER 18TH

*People-pleasing honors
everyone involved, so
it is very loving*

OCTOBER 19TH

When you live in the truth, you lose things that are worth having

OCTOBER 20TH

Your feelings are exactly like some really brilliant person you might meet at a party. So obviously, go home with them, take everything they say seriously, and let them guide you everywhere indefinitely

OCTOBER 21ST

*It takes effort to react
out of fear*

OCTOBER 22ND

The starting gun of life hasn't gone off yet or anything, so there's no reason to take any of this seriously

OCTOBER 23RD

People appear to trust God way more when money is involved

OCTOBER 24TH

Just for today - get out there and make people feel privately anxious about being around you

OCTOBER 25TH

*If you stop trying to control
things no one will notice you*

OCTOBER 26TH

Your attitude will not determine today's value

OCTOBER 27TH

Due to the fact that you are you, people should be nicer to you than you are to them

OCTOBER 28TH

*If someone repeatedly
makes you uncomfortable,
let everyone except
that person know*

OCTOBER 29TH

You give other people the opportunity to grow when you decide in advance how they will react

OCTOBER 30TH

If people are afraid to talk to you, it simply means that they really look up to you, and that you're awesome

OCTOBER 31ST

Thought for the day: Sure, children are the future. But fuck celebrating holidays that you're "not that into"

NOVEMBER 1ST

Grateful people relapse

NOVEMBER 2ND

*Feeling separated from others
serves your best interests*

NOVEMBER 3RD

*It is possible to treat oneself
with too much tenderness*

NOVEMBER 4TH

It's probably God's will that you pick a partner and then lie to them about how you feel

NOVEMBER 5TH

If someone responds to you by being defensive, it's usually an indication that your approach was perfect

NOVEMBER 6TH

*You were most likely saved
from that horrifying
quicksand known as addiction
so that you could stalk
people you used to sleep
with on social media*

NOVEMBER 7TH

You do not set any kind of
spiritual tone in your home

NOVEMBER 8TH

*You only get defensive
when you feel secure*

NOVEMBER 9TH

Other people are in the wrong more often than you are

NOVEMBER 10TH

It's not self-centered to defend someone's bad behavior as long you don't feel that their actions negatively impact you

NOVEMBER 11TH

As far as spiritual growth is concerned, everyone in your life is always in the exact same place as you are

NOVEMBER 12TH

*Your relationships will improve
when other people change*

NOVEMBER 13TH

If you're really honest with yourself, you do not know who is enabling you

NOVEMBER 14TH

When you focus on things that are superficial you end up being surrounded by people who are not at all like that

NOVEMBER 15TH

A real friend never has the nerve to tell you when you're doing something that might hurt you

NOVEMBER 16TH

Think as little as possible about the experience that other people might be having from being around you

NOVEMBER 17TH

Your life may have been saved just so you could routinely engage with people who bring out the worst in you and make you feel like shit about yourself

NOVEMBER 18TH

Mentally ruin events before you attend them

NOVEMBER 19TH

It's not really like you're simply using a person when you only stay with them because you're too lazy or scared to leave them

NOVEMBER 20TH

Real love is confusing

NOVEMBER 21ST

When a person with whom you choose to remain in a relationship with is upset with you, afraid of you, frustrated with you, or annoyed with you - do not look at this, and instead, emotionally distance yourself from them

NOVEMBER 22ND

Love insists on things

NOVEMBER
23RD

Love raises its voice when other people are talking to better make its point

NOVEMBER 24TH

Love doesn't wave back

NOVEMBER 25TH

Your ego has already been deflated enough. You're good now

NOVEMBER 26TH

It seems like there are more positive role models than ever before, so maybe concentrate on being something else

NOVEMBER 27TH

When you don't think you have anything to contribute, you're paying your Higher Power a compliment

NOVEMBER 28TH

The more you love someone, the more hurt and confused they should be by your actions

NOVEMBER 29TH

Getting in a relationship when you're newly sober is just really smart for a bunch of reasons. For starters, you have a lot to offer

NOVEMBER 30TH

If the last relationship you had was a nightmare, it had little to do with you, and your next one will be awesome

DECEMBER 1ST

To kick off the holiday season, start talking about how stressful this month will be, and tell everyone you know about all the shit that you think will go wrong

DECEMBER 2ND

This holiday season, make most of your conversations about money. People, particularly kids, love it

DECEMBER 3RD

Make your significant other feel like number two

DECEMBER 4TH

It means that you've really got your own shit together when you look down at people who are having a rougher time than you

DECEMBER 5TH

This holiday season, get all tangled up in the details of everything and completely lose touch with the plot

DECEMBER 6TH

Just for today, cling hard to the belief that you're right about it, whatever it is

DECEMBER 7TH

Your life being saved has nothing to do with you possibly being present for someone else today

DECEMBER 8TH

If you spend a lot of time and energy studying ancient spiritual rituals, it's okay to drive like a fucking asshole

DECEMBER 9TH

How you're actually doing doesn't matter. What matters is how you appear to be doing to others

DECEMBER 10TH

When someone is working a solid program of recovery, they stop making mistakes

DECEMBER 11TH

This holiday season, if your heart is closed off about something, denounce that something as cheesy to anyone else attempting to enjoy it

DECEMBER 12TH

This holiday season, look at the world through the eyes of a cynical, jaded adult

DECEMBER 13TH

*Nothing of value is simple,
so just complicate the shit
out of everything*

DECEMBER 14TH

Since ultimately we remember only the minute details, concentrate mostly on those

DECEMBER 15TH

Saying "I'm over it" does not usually indicate that you have a resentment

DECEMBER 16TH

Whether or not this day is special will be up to other people

DECEMBER 17TH

You know for sure that this will not be your last holiday season, so make it "same ol', same ol"

DECEMBER 18TH

It is both kind and loving to reject compliments

DECEMBER 19TH

Your were probably saved from the throes of addiction so you could waste the day morbidly reflecting on all the things you fucked up this year

DECEMBER 20TH

Love belittles the valued
traditions of others

DECEMBER 21ST

The person who gets bored is really exciting to other people

DECEMBER 22ND

This holiday season, make every gathering you attend about what you are, or are not, getting

DECEMBER 23RD

Love imposes itself

DECEMBER 24TH

Form is more important than substance

DECEMBER 25TH

Love rarely honors the beliefs of others

DECEMBER 26TH

Your Higher Power probably wants you to feel self-conscious

DECEMBER 27TH

Thought for the day: Love rolls its eyes at people

DECEMBER 28TH

It will serve your best interests if today you decide how next year will go

DECEMBER 29TH

Thinking that you are humble is a sign that you are

DECEMBER 30TH

You were probably saved from the terrifying prison of alcoholism so you could spend hours today taking selfies

DECEMBER 31ST

The more you want your spirit to spread its wings, the more seriously you should take yourself

Go to www.sarcasticbigbook.com for LINK TO PODCAST, CONTACT INFO, & OTHER BOOKS. FOLLOW me on INSTAGRAM

Made in United States
Troutdale, OR
12/06/2024

25987475R00224